An Undergrowth of Myth-making

Alex Hand

An Undergrowth of Myth-making

Acknowledgements

'Argon' and 'Tired of Meteorologists' clichés' appeared in
Dawntreader,
Soil in Time chapbook by Ginninderra Press,
'Woman with tattoos' in *Quadrant*,
'Without my specs' in *Sisyphus*,
'Retuned' in *Stories from the Heart, Misnomer in My Inside Voice*,
'Garden' in *From the Edge*,
'White sesame seeds about two pounds' in *Orbis*.

'Oldies', First place, Southport Writers' Circle Annual International
Poetry Competition 2020

Christine, thank you for being such a patient sounding board for my constant barrage of questions. Your comments are invaluable. Thank you too to Anne Lewis for such pedantic and painstaking proofreading of my work..

For
Christine, Sebastian and Rachel

An Undergrowth of Myth-making
ISBN 978 1 76109 466 8
Copyright © text Alex Hand 2023
Cover image from PxHere

First published 2023 by
GINNINDERRA PRESS
PO Box 3461 Port Adelaide 5015
www.ginninderrapress.com.au

Contents

A sort of dakhma	7
Paper	8
Italian tomatoes	9
Wet wood beacon	11
Well dressing	12
Bulldog clip	14
To dance	15
Wildflower meadows	16
A stained glass imagining	17
Close to the heart	18
The Queensland Magpie taught Maria Callas to sing	19
Intelligent idleness	20
Tracking the thoughts of others	21
Somehow	22
Crow	23
Cyril	25
A decent politician	26
Smoke	28
Tired of meteorologists' clichés	29
Potash	31
Argon	33
Without specs	34
To arms	35
St Mary's Church	37
Church	38
Church no more	39
What a party	40
Garden	41
Seeds	42
Without a GPS	43

Unknown neighbours	45
Souterraine champignon	46
Gods and none	47
Hildegard of Bingen	48
Not a drop	49
Rain after three years	51
On the farm	52
Oldies	53
Turfing	54
Twenty-four hours in the tropics	55
Woman with tattoos	56
Self-portrait	57
Strong is how he likes his drinks	59
Pint of mild please	60
Misnomer	61
2020 – City centre in absentia	62
Retuned	63
Standing	64
Elegant sufficiency	66
Change of collar and continent	67
Changing Services	68
Night-time life	69
George Street Wind Tunnel	71
White sesame seeds about two pounds	72
Bury me	74

A sort of dakhma

A skink lay on a letter box,
draped across the hinge.
It was dead and drying,
mostly grey but albescent.
It reminded me of two things:
a lightly fried sardine with
silversmith fine white bones
and how, unlike gekkotans,
we are basically bags of water.

>When my body stops functioning
there'll be a leak of fluids,
and the slow loss of shape
like an air mattress with a puncture.
Silk and eco-friendly fibreboard
will only hinder my disintegration,
and unlike that lizard I saw
I shall neither be beauty
nor immediate use to bacteria.

Had I taken that featherweight
and interned it in soil,
just an inch or two deep,
would I have caused hunger
in a colony of letterbox-dwelling ants?
Perhaps better to simply meditate,
to stare a little
and assume that carnivorous fellow
had a reasonable life.

Paper

For months I hadn't written to Mum,
with only intentions of a phone call.

I searched for locally made writing paper,
I could have used something straight off the shelf
but if I'm writing it has to be meaningful.
Found Gwen in the next suburb, Redhill,
making paper like a Fabriano artisan
like a new age suburban sole trader.
She called herself a papermaker, a little dull
I far preferred the title *papetier*, French of course;
either way, flecked with fluff, she welcomed me in.
There was a showroom big as a newspaper kiosk
and immediately I was in sensory overload,
opaque tissue, ivory vellum and wrapping paper,
with leafy, barky smells and rose petal sweetness.
I said I wanted a few sheets to write to my mother,
a parchment equivalent of Michelin five stars I got;
my eyes settled on exquisite paper with wattle seeds
the golden flowers pressed into the quire, flattened.
My mother's eyes were old, more blind than seeing
she would miss the beauty of the artistry, for sure,
but that's fine. It's the time I took hunting it down,
the novelty of finding what's in my own backyard.
Mum will have someone read her the words I write,
touching that paper though, she'll sense me there.

Italian tomatoes

We moved in where an Italian couple had lived,
they must have been there since the year dot.
Well-behaved and highly pruned orange trees
stood as testament to the pair's garden life.

Beside the garage were two terracotta pots,
with pale green lichen on both like life stains.
In one an overflow of dainty purple petunias
and in the second a sprawling tomato plant.

More hirsute than an average tomato stem,
its stalk gnarled and knobbed like an oak tree
but green as young broccoli and wet coriander;
it wound itself loosely round a ten-foot cane.

Elegantly calligraphed in silver on the clay pot,
in old Sicilian, *'acqua con grappa, canta Bellini'*.
My finger traced the lines of writing curiously,
mouthing softly, 'water with grappa, sing Bellini'.

I played Maria Callas singing *Norma* from Bellini
then watched the tomato plant ripple in time,
and poured grappa in a clear threadlike stream
from an old fluted champagne glass, into the pot.

The vine belly danced and fondled its way up
shaking the lilac yesterday, today and tomorrow,
up onto the corrugated garage roof and sat there.
For a week it sat, soaking up the midday heat.

I replayed that exquisite aria to the moist roots
and finger flicked a few more drops of spirit;
white hairs flicked their scent right back at me,
quivering like a butterfly correcting its flight.

Stems clung on to the tin roof and stole across,
tickling the galvanised sheets almost audibly.
The first yellow flowers peeped over the side
young leaves followed and unfurled purposefully.

On the northward side of the garage, it dropped
with parcels of dried red fruit like large goji.
On their journey clusters of lime green balls
had reddened turning into sun-dried tomatoes.

Those succulent sun-dried tomatoes dawdled on,
hanging like wisteria but in autumn colours.
We picked until we'd filled ten dinner plates
and ate them with *pane pugliese* and light wine.

Beside the garden shed another large flower pot
etched into it in looping curly script two lines
in some early Dalmatian predecessor of Italian,
of which all I could guess was the word 'vino'.

Wet wood beacon

Longboats on the horizon,
oarsmen's salty bodies
pull them landwards,
Valhalla ferments inside.

On all fours I blow
on the glowing embers
grabbing handfuls of twigs
and blocking the wind.

The tinder's damp,
it smoulders, it's obstinate.
Smoke washes my eyes,
no salvation flames.

The beacon waits unlit,
cinders deny me any hope
and rebuff sobbing entreaties.
My hammering heart rages.

Bearded beasts jump ashore,
wave after wave.
One raises his axe high
and hews me like timber.

He rocks it violently,
pulls it from my ribcage,
my innards spew sluggishly out,
blood percolates in the embers.

He walks on, voices follow.
The footfalls of fate dull now.
My lifeblood drains away,
no soul ascending, silence.

Well dressing

In England some folk in the north dress wells,
an intricate act of veneration, the origins moot.
The custom may pre-date the Romans' arrival
or stem from boreal denizen in darker ages.

A fissure in the rocks where water flowed,
a local fountainhead and built village wells;
here the locals came and echoing antiquity
as common artificers, they created dressings.

Some resembled a tufty moss-coated buttercross
others were like rampant floral mantelpieces.
As with bygone hazel and birch broom makers
and bee skep stitchers, such skills are bequeathed.

From locally-hewn trees they built a wooden frame,
mixed wetted clay and salt to cover the timber.
In drying clod one pair of hands crafted a homage
to a local deity in earlier times, biblical thereafter.

From their thorp and woodland, they gathered;
each brought cushions of dark green moss and
baskets of flower petals, all indigenous blooms.
Lads brought seed pods, fir cones and fonds too.

Together, with common purpose, they worked,
villagers filled the impression with their flowerage;
laid like gemstones, filigree silver and gold leaf
the sweet-smelling harvest from their surrounds.

The water source was dressed from the land,
pale yellow primroses, sweet lily-of-the-valley,
wood anemone, dainty harebell and foxglove
with curled fern fonds and soft common moss.

Bloodshot field poppies they added for effect,
petite scarlet pimpernels as elegant highlights.
Cold hard granite evolved to be so much more,
adorned with the garnish from the fertile earth.

Whether the reverence paid was just the creation
or incantations, perhaps prayers too, is unknown.
When flowers had wilted and blossoms shrivelled
the village broke it apart for compost and renewal.

Bulldog clip

A bulldog clip placed on these papers a hundred years ago
by an admin clerk in an uninviting public servant's office,
at an ink-stained desk with barely a sign of previous occupants.
The issue typed up on the papers long since trivialised,
two generations since the people named were walking.
Ploughed up, subdivided and built on with no permanence,
the land has ceased to stir emotion in any one heart.
But the bulldog clip has not been dismissed until now;
for this past century it has stayed in place, locked in duty,
like solid roots of an ancient tree holding the earth in place.
There's a thumb print on the bulldog clip, a swathe of DNA,
and should a genealogist choose they could reconstruct the clerk,
build her life history, track her employment and call her by her name.
Today those papers are unclasped from the tight embrace,
that bulldog clip is dropped into a bin by a spendthrift office wallah,
history undone, and curiosity an unpaid and unwanted tick.
The clip will rust for a decade or two in a landfill site,
the papers will be shredded by in-confidence commercial shredders,
and the clerk shuffled off her earthly coil long since, forgotten by all.

To dance

To have a sense of rhythm,
an affinity with vibrations,
beautiful; but my shortcoming.

With a South American twirl,
or a Greek instinctive step,
others seem attuned to life.

I appreciate their appetite,
their taste for spontaneity,
their exquisite movement.

With Elgar's cello concerto
in E minor, an English fiddle,
or Rossini's William Tell Overture,

I transcend the mundane
with otherworldly ease
but I just lack any swing.

Wildflower meadows

In the midst of sprawling Berlin,
the heart of the Bundesrepublik,
thrive fifty wildflower meadows.

The council created rustic scenes
in the capital of Europe's powerhouse,
micro wildernesses in suburbs and city.

It dug up tidy parks of clipped lawns
and seeded them with careful purpose,
jumbled and anarchic to the urban eye.

There are native flowers in full bloom,
the endangered species' inflorescence
resemble pre-industrialised grasslands.

These Arcadian throwbacks flamboyant,
the endemic meadows in stunning colours;
sown for endangered bees, of sundry types.

Solitary native bees *bombinate en bloc,*
with miner bees burrowing like badgers
and the pollen rich lea tempting to each.

A social experiment in wilding apiculture,
where poppies and wild grass are hostesses
to bees, gently pulling them from extinction.

Blowing through built-up Berlin
the scent of honey and wispy feminine notes,
as bees suck at sweet nectaries; a blithe sight.

A stained glass imagining

From the third floor the treetops are filigree fine,
emergent tendrils nod nervously
in the breath of a gossamer breeze.
Lace leaves play like piano fingers
caught by ripples from whippish curlicue.

The street lights glare a little more furiously
as the ashen sky becomes leaden, stygian.
Doorways swell in deepening shadow
with a nativity calendar of yellow windows
as a five-minute winter hovers broodingly.

Stained glass windows in the clerestories
of Norman or Gothic cathedrals
hold the devotee or casual onlooker absorbed.
A glazier with a cathedralic brief
sweats his soul into his magnum opus.

But here from this vantage point, I see
a secular masterpiece in the making.
Man-made environment and nature synergetic
and by the chemistry of light and shade
I am simply mesmerised, enraptured.

Close to the heart

After the cremation he took the urn to a tattoo parlour,
there he had the grey ashes mixed with cobalt pigment.
The tattooist emblazoned a life-size portrait on his chest;
today the husband's wife shares his flannelette pyjamas.

The Queensland Magpie taught Maria Callas to sing

In the undergrowth of myth-making could this not be true;
because the mezzo-soprano in the white frangipani tree
sings sublime arias spiralling lazily in the sultry dog-days.
For twenty years, the garden's hosted the magpie's tiding,
its kith and kin, with heads arched back gurgling sweetly.
Black and white to embarrass a well-pressed dinner suit,
it launches into an *arietta*, flute-like and rapturous, inviting –
a duet partner always replies, together quite otherworldly.
Two dozen magpies, with a matriarchal territory to defend,
sing such complex songs, with cousins and aunties joining,
forgive the slight anthropomorphism, but that's literally so.
This songbird not to be confused with its British namesake,
each from distinctly different genus, separated through time.
The Australian magpie is endowed with a tell-tale sobriquet,
less often used but with figurative honesty, the 'Flute Bird';
an epithet unknown to Mozart, he oblivious to its magic voice.
The crimson rosella and musk lorikeet gorgeous colours;
but the Queensland magpie is by any measure quite divine,
a songbird whose transcendental voice is solo, choral – pure.

Intelligent idleness

Apprenticed to a sartorial *flâneur,*
I'm upskilling to dutiful indolence,
watching moss grow and time flow.

I seek to savour the quiddity of being,
to touch the marrow of colliding atoms,
and to surpass the master at *flânerie.*

The hours are long and capricious;
I pore over the unsleeping landscape
and sew my soul into the pure vocation.

A dog-eared copy of *Battling the Gods*
sits in my lap; under eminent tutelage
I engage with life at a conducive pace.

Tracking the thoughts of others

Sitting in the Bodleian, doing research,
not scholarly but bordering on madness,
the difference is fine, the chase sublime.
Marginalia found me in our local library,
in fact, in *The Australian Book of Atheism,*
lying in my right hand, as I leafed with my left.
A reader had used a 4H pencil in the gutter;
softly written, now a ghost of its intention,
she had referenced a labyrinth of thinkers.
There was Anaximander and Cleanthes,
and frequently Meister Eckhart and Spinoza,
with Claude Debussy alongside Paul Harrison.
Like Alice minus blue bows and ivory pinafore,
I tumbled down an unending rabbit hole
into a *purlieu* where codes and clarity mingled.
Accompanying each name were summations,
glosses, exclamation marks, two-way arrows,
titles, editions, dates and page numbers.
The encipher's world of inner thought palpable,
not the domain of purely the physical senses,
but the whole spectrum of bodily cognition;
and that is why I am in this hallowed bibliotheca.
Unlike a detective who seeks but one prey,
mine is a search in countless directions
following names until they lead to a juncture,
sliding between the exoteric and esoteric.
I found that dipping the toe leads to immersion,
that one scribble can be insanely beguiling.
I have not touched my graphite to any margin,
instead, I have filled acres of notebooks,
this as a strange antithesis to my avocation.

Somehow

A brilliant blue sky,
each day warmer,
scarlet hibiscuses
mesmerise and impress.
Nasturtium flowers
of saffron and cerise,
delicate and dainty.
Matisse's philosophy
is simple cheerfulness
to battle the misery
of a material life.
But, how to be cheerful
in a year of Covid,
with legs kicked away
from under you,
the structure of the usual
recklessly deconstructed.
With a desolation of data,
to make choices is tortuous,
to be blind to the bewitchery
of the back garden easy.
To animate current drudgery
with a Matisse state of mind,
is as good a guiding star
as any in this cinerary present.

Crow

It's been left, or didn't go,
a crow with white eyes
pomaded plumage
and what feels like ubiquity.

Hopping like a *bouffon*,
sideways, forwards
then launching clumsily;
yet there's grace in its erratic bouncing.

For months it's been alone,
joining us on the patio,
finishing the cats' leftovers,
cawing, perhaps for a long-gone murder.

One morning, two crows,
either siblings or a potential twosome;
no puffed chests, no territory dispute.
But cautious early amorosity perchance.

Now that solitary adoptee
shows he's male,
but his gauche attempts at ritual
show a kink in his congenital memory.

Not quite offering
an untaught interpretation
of paternal mating routine, with swagger;
he flounces, he gambols; almost caprine.

Between the mandibles
an inch of needle-thin straw,
intended as a wooing prop,
for this male, though, it becomes a *marotte*.

Then he's alone, again.
Are they a dryad,
is she with child?
His appetite has grown, with luck for three.

Cyril

Cyril stands in the garden reading Richard Dawkins to the afternoon,
and when he's in a more lyrical mood he reads Auden or Virgil instead.
The rocket and radishes along the driveway remain silent as he reads,
while the blue-faced honeyeater, the banana bird, heckles noisily
but the butcher bird, more polite, will listen for five solid minutes.

The neighbours think him odd. The cats, though, don't agree;
they'll wind their afternoon round him like curly passion fruit tendrils.
Odd would be sharing Dawkins with the morning, regardless of mood,
when all around is unfurling, frantic and deaf and caffeine-bound.
At four p.m. it's time for Pimm's or a floral gin, the sun slowly ebbing.

A decent politician

Name five decent politicians!
Celia challenged Jim,
adding a bit of fencing.
Someone who doesn't simply perpetuate the status quo,
a mind which sees we're all tenants on earth,
erudite with a common touch,
has vision but understands the past.
Can you do that?

Jim stared with his big brown bovine eyes
straight into Celia's eyes;
thinking.

Jacinda Ardern,
he said as if the answer rose in the east and set in the west,
as if bleedin' obvious was standing beside the two of them.

And?
Celia waited.
She waited,
waited;
her Gaelic red hair silvering daily,
waiting.

Jim lives in the library,
grappling with Nordic governments,
scouring African leaders,
looking for the second name,
looking, wanting so bloomin' badly.

He grows old and physically frail,
gaunt with failure,
his chestnut eyes shelled,
with Aneurin Bevan on the tip of his tongue.

And?
Celia asks,
not hopeful
but wishing.

His last breath seeped between his lips,
a cold wizen gasp,
'No.'

Before she wrote his epitaph
before laying him to rest
she whispered across his ashen face;
'you didn't have to spend your life answering,
you didn't have to answer
you didn't.'

Smoke

Smoke from the neighbours' garden
floats over the fence in purple wisps
curls around the almost dry washing
hanging static on the whirligig line.

Josephine leaves it for the night time
to leave its scent of dew-flecked grass
and balmy hawthorn petals emitting
spice long after stripey bees are gone.

Tired of meteorologists' clichés

Forecasters predict five days of mild-mannered storms;
tempered winds smelling of jasmine and sea salt,
bring swirling negative ions, fresh courtesies of Aura.

A deft embroidering of the coastline wheat fields
and goat willow swiftly crocheted, with fluffy yellow
flowers wedded to the tied knots on lithe branches.

Apologetic gusts commandeer the sash windows
of the pub whose rusty sign does somersaults,
while the crates of empty beer bottles percuss.

And the sky which should be getting dark and heavy
can only manage a threatening off-white sombreness
which feels like coils of rice paper and rolled oats.

But nonetheless they rumble when they bump,
not a Wagnerian rumble but the slow vibrations
of a cello sonata strung by a master *luthier*.

And there's a hush surrounding this sensuousness,
which highlights it more when it comes, the D-string
intimate with the earthly pairs of skyward eyes.

Lightning flashes fall in a lackadaisical manner,
the perfect antithesis of a sewing machine needle,
curling up on impact and coiling to a tired standstill.

Raindrops plop like wet meringues making coronets
and before the driblets settle more drops crash down
in easy succession strumming the inky tarmac.

The late surreal afternoon a euphonious display of
of what meteorologists are loath to say on air,
that storms, with imagination, need not be severe.

Potash

Under the shipping lanes
where Russian ships spy
bulk carriers crawl
and frigates patrol,
beneath churning waves
and waning schools of fish,
deep below the seabed
miners dig for potash.

Way out in the North Sea,
in the nether depths
of Davy Jones's locker
a mile deep,
borers cut tunnels
burrow galleries
follow loaded seams,
claw farther outwards.

Inside the sunken workings
the belly of the shaft
bowels of the Anthropocene
it's Bangkok hot,
close heat hugs
mimics the tropics
enfolds the pitmen
slows the timeless day.

From the first excavations
the passages through ore
shore up of roofs
in moving mineral strata,
as potash walls warp
they sag and slump
buckle and flow,
mine maps modify daily.

Far from sailors' thoughts,
unseen from those above
in surroundings that move
where the inanimate drifts,
miners earn the potash
gut the chambers
haul the prize
for farmers' overhead.

Argon

Every breath I take contains argon atoms from daVinci's lungs,
from the musing of Steven Rose, I inhale iotas of helium,
the screams of my ancestral mothers, giving birth, are in my breath.
As I sleep, I respire oxygen molecules emitted from the
edelweiss in Switzerland,
from the seaweed in the Pacific, from my neighbour's lawn.
In an ordinary day I consume volcanoes and beating hearts,
I breathe in and out physical history.
In a thousand years, others will breathe in some part of me;
I shall be antiquity in the veins of your descendants.

Without specs

The good thing about needing glasses and not wearing them is that you can't see the weevils in the besan flour, or even the digits on the bathroom scales, inferring instead that all is well.

A certain beauty of forgetting to put the glasses on is that red, white and blue of any flag you like becomes a grandmotherly purple and quite difficult to be patriotic about.

And the best time to forget your specs is election time when each party's political placards are indistinguishable from each other's which has a certain irony.

Without glasses I see three moons or rather crescents overlapping like all for one and one for all with Arabian scimitars, and certainly as good as other peoples' moon, through glasses.

There's value in failing to pick up the glasses and not sitting them on the bridge of the nose because the night sky becomes so much abstract art, the possibilities endless with new shapes failing miserably to focus perched in the cusp of different mythologies.

Torn between slipping the glasses on or not; dithering – the two rain forest birds carry a gorgeous duet but are invisible, saffron dahlias in a bunch of three glow like a hilltop beacon but all that's seen is blob of yellow.

Intentionally watching the news glassless and it's odd how things in the world seem so much better.

To arms

To bear arms is wrong, albeit well-caveated.
Not from a quaker's perspective do I say this
but from clear as day manifest common-sense.

The populace belongs in the agora, feet planted,
take that as a place where ideas are exchanged
where the sweaty and the perfumed rub shoulders.

Being sentient and alive to the pain of living,
searching like pilgrims for daily contentedness,
ordinary folk make meaning for themselves.

They join the dots when they see them,
they have an innate sense of what's right
and just don't live in a dog-eat-dog world.

Citizens, not subjects, but citizens, talk,
they talk together, sometimes over each other,
but they talk, and repeatedly assert their views.

When justice is more than blind, but deaf too,
when the multitude of little people are ignored,
the public feel trickle down liberticide, again.

Peterloo still haunts and hangs in the psyche,
Merthyr Rising was simply a plea for fair wages,
and the anger of the Battle of Orgreave remains.

In such cases where swords and hooves kill,
where lead shot was fired with one intention,
and the heavy-handed state bludgeons miners.

In such cases, is it, after all, wrong to bear arms?
Firearms not by choice, not even conceivable
but, when neighbours die for the vote or bread.

Further afield the question is no less valid,
surely the Myanmarese would be asking,
as those whose burden is Bolsonaro's apathy.

To bear arms is wrong, in a civilised society
unequivocally, from an enlightened perspective.
And if those paid to protect do not…

St Mary's Church

Between the technical college and the Masons Arms
was a shaded path greased with slippery wet leaves;
it ran through church grounds, home to burnt-out winos.
The grassed area with forlorn headstones was thigh high,
the sides of the path built-up so it felt like a neat trench.

Tech students traipsed the pathway in chatting huddles
past the Anglican church of weathered Purbeck stone,
on Hamwic history and consecrated ground since AD 634.
They walked with neither reverence nor irreverence
but in nescience and flared denims, pulled by a waiting pint

Church

The church in the next village is small and solid,
dating back to some rudimentary monk.
At the door, the step is truly worn down
through unswerving footfalls over millennia,
rubbing it away, polished into a smooth caldera.
An hour away by car there's a cathedral,
with exquisite spires, ecru against the grey sky
purportedly for funnelling prayers to their maker.
The stained-glass windows stop you dead,
if you aren't awe-struck, you aren't animate.
But somehow that eroded church doorstep
is the thing that tugs at me, confounds me;
I wonder about those billions of micro particles,
the finest powder of stone brushed by leather
and swept into the narthex, into the cool sanctum.

Church no more

The two blue doors of Eumundi church are closed,
deconsecration of the site has been performed,
and the final turn of the key aired on the news.

Its congregation has dried up to just a handful
like the creeks and dams around, all dry;
the Word brings neither believers nor rain.

It's the most ungodly suburb in Queensland,
a factual statement, this time, from the minister,
as recent censuses show, religious affiliation's down.

The Gympie messmate pews lined up for sale,
stroked wistfully by a romantic ecclesiologist
imagining the families who prayed year-on-year.

Christian artefacts lie disused, unfriended,
bibles packed in boxes labelled 'mission Africa',
the freight costs waiting for a benevolent angel.

Soon to be auctioned rather than simply sold,
after all, it's the last of its kind, in Eumundi;
whoever buys it will have many gentle guests.

What a party

I threw some bread crusts to a solitary crow.
Eighteen magpies had a gatecrashers' party.
The crow and I exchanged glances and went
Our separate   ways.

Garden

I know the name of virtually nothing in the garden
but we're on more than just nodding terms.

When I do talk, I slide from chatting with the cats
to sometimes calling the lemon grass poppet

In an absent-minded way, the cat oblivious, I think.
Mostly though I articulate little, intentionally.

Sometimes there's the odd dialogue, verbalised;
an observer would be forgiven for thinking it a soliloquy.

We commune in silence, semi-religious in a natural way,
sharing, and I'm always on the receiving end.

I could walk the garden twelve dozen times
and still forget their names, classified in Latin

Working down from order, family, genus, species,
not so important. Ceres and I, we get on well.

Seeds

Her garden is not particularly large –
in fact, it's almost nooks and crannies.

But it holds you in its petal lights,
with a paltry lexicon of appreciation.

She's a seed-grabber, discreetly so,
a Fagin of every existing shrubbery.

She'll walk home buried in shopping,
unfurl her fingers to expose dry kernels;

Fingers of an haute-couture virtuoso
when filching other's dry brown seed.

Walking down the driveway is akin to
a slow release from deep meditation.

Not a penny spent on over-the-counter,
deeply invested in a constellation of muse.

Without a GPS

Grandad gave directions with pubs;
'Turn left at the Red Lion, go as far as the Masons Arms,
then cross the road and walk until you get to the Bugle.
If you reach the Fox and Hounds you've gone too far.'
Wasn't much help if you weren't near the Red Lion to start.

For Mum, it was the toilets;
'In Banbury at the end of the car park there're clean loos
and also, in the Abingdon Waitrose at the back of the restaurant.
As soon as you get to Witney go straight to the woollen mills,
they do lovely coffee and eclairs and they have good toilets too.'

But – Milly- didn't have a mappy mind, no spatial intelligence;
her 'turn left' would be couched in doubt and chancy hesitation,
and 'a little further', whether miles or metres, was always suspect.
Landmarks, should she offer any, were little more than conjecture.
She generally used taxis to get about, and was often taken for a ride.

Dave's effort at directions was far more down to earth.
'Along the A30 until you see the pleached hedges ahead,
left by the old barn on staddle stones that's collapsing
and just keep going till you get to a monkey puzzle tree,
there's a little table with eggs for sale just before you arrive.'

And Sarah's directions, well, they were purely anatomical.
'When you hear those biplanes buzzing about, look for Alton,
you can sometimes feel the rumble of tanks on exercises nearby.
You'll smell the airport from miles away, with the kerosene fuel,
the air prickles your nostrils and feels different, sort of jetty-like.'

Esme, she knew places in her feet first and later in her head;
the thing is, she'd always walked everywhere, or cycled
and any directions she gave were footpaths or bridleways,
through churchyards and the routes with gentler gradients.
Her directions though, sort of vulpine-level, were the best.

Unknown neighbours

Everyday Mr Riley cycles home,
in flat cap and bicycle clips.
Plodding rhythmically –
a leaden pace,
marginally faster than me.
Each day of my school life,
and probably before,
he creaked along.
I never knew for sure;
just assumed it was to work.

Souterraine champignon

Beneath the awnings of Parisienne cafés,
the cobbled stones and cool wine cellars,
under the feet of *Liberté, égalité, fraternité*
there was a godless great mushroom farm.

For three centuries Paris had a quarry,
fathers and sons toiled in candlelit darkness
until the seams of limestone ran dry.
They were hypogean quarrymen no more.

Two thousand men worked the horse manure,
from breathing rock dust to mushroom spores;
their new bread and butter was fungiculture –
an innovative existence without pickaxe or fear.

They left a stone legacy for France's monuments
a hollowness like a massive uncharted black hole.
They left a yawning expanse for surveyors to classify
and an underground hideaway for the lawless.

Before the mushrooms and after the digging
came the bones; fleshless, both recent and ancient,
disinterred from the city's decrepit cemeteries,
and led from churchyards by Catholic priests.

Sealed away like the wine of Santa Vittoria,
skulls with their sockets all looking westwards
and bones with marrow long lost to the earth.
A mass exhumation by order of King Louis XVI.

Gods and none

In the past local gods were known here.
This river, where ancient Britons dumped their bronze,
had its own deity
and there was an indigenous god of fertility,
to whom not just farmers but all who could
would pay homage.

Now there are just godless locals,
whose life is lived in binary, believer or atheist,
as if that's all there is.
For them no nuanced shades of thought between,
no inkling that most ideas are fuzzy at the edges;
there's just today.

Sliding headfirst into a midwife's hands;
that's arguably the first connection the little life makes
of unlimited connectedness.
Be it the garrulous storm or the ground beneath,
the lustrous night sky or your own inbred accent;
you can't deny there's relatedness.

Hildegard of Bingen

composed canticles in the twelfth century,
psalms to melodies, in self-taught style,
this mystic's melismatic chants stop my car.
Something about her seeps deep into me
trickles through me in numinous affection,
her verses to God flow across eight centuries
quite absurdly angelic to my material world.

Not a drop

Went to give blood,
'Been to the UK?'
I had.

'Bovine spongiform encephalopathy
in the food chain.'
My pint declined.

'I'm a vegetarian,
no mad cow in me.'
'It's in the food chain.'

'I'm vegan,
not a drop of milk passed my lips.'
'Deep in the food chain,' same refrain.

'Not a morsel of beef,
not a drop of milk.'
But tainted, I was.

'Thanks, but no,
been to the UK, see,
can't take it.'

'So, the English blood banks,
all closed up?'
No answer.

A, B, O, positive;
don't know,
first time, civic duty.

Ovine spinal cord
fed to cows,
herbivores they are, were.

Maddened now,
by crossing nature,
crossing the line.

Red Cross caravan
in Brisbane, 'stralia,
part of the UK food chain, see.

Rain after three years

Aged three, sees rain for the first time;
its smell, its harmonic throbbing –
a farrago of innocent confusion.
Locke's empiricism in three dimensions.

The dog, for hopeless months
was lethargic and dusty, now
runs circles round its own delirium,
teaching the toddler to splash madly.

Fissured earth, the creek impoverished,
grass desiccated into its own misery;
then black clouds roll in and over,
answering prayers and atheists alike.

Yesterday a cartography of repossession
today a filthy salvation.
Fully clothed – completely sane,
dancing, falling and blithely being.

On the farm

For summer holidays we camped at Uncle Harry's farm
halfway between Chadlington and Charlbury,
both huddled villages tucked into the Cotswolds countryside
and standing witness to changing life cycles of village folk.

We built a dam with mud and sticks across a peaceful stream
between two fields, one of wheat the other lying fallow,
our fingers delved into sediment; our feet planted midstream.
The last one we made had pretensions of wattle and daub.

Harry delivered pig feed in hefty jute sacks, to piggeries
and swineherds, in his Trafalgar blue Austin van;
we scrambled on top, carefree, jumping out at each farm.
Then stopped in Chipping Norton for fish and chips.

Draped over the gate, we watched the flock bottleneck.
I thought the sheep with their green smit marks foolish,
but our two Jack Russells couldn't get enough of them;
the ovine churned mud covered both, to their sheer delight.

One time we walked single file along the country lanes
to a cascading and overladen elderberry tree;
there we stretched and picked and pulled, till we had
gorgeous purple stains and Dad could make his wine.

For breakfast we had the freshest eggs possible,
cooked outdoors on a primus stove, it smelt so good.
At night, we'd roll our clothes up for a pillow,
and sleep to open sky noises and tired Jack Russells.

Oldies

Two oldies on the corner of the road, holding hands, in verbal silence.
The grand narratives of humanity long since interrogated,
now it's down to the unspoken word and functional language – Tea?
He in an old flat cap, she well dressed and neither with a nod to today.

To the untrained eye they are a couple from a bygone age,
morose and probably smelling of mothballs and mildew.
But neither body nor mind gather a smidgen of moss;
she has green fingers; he loves his history hardbacks.

From the back to see the over sixties holding hands, gorgeous,
decade after decade the same familiar coupling of fingers.
Between them they finish the *Guardian* crossword in fifteen minutes
and think the private thoughts of ageing slowly.

Turfing

Bare patches of earth expand where lawn once was.
Runners of grass creep like bald men's combed hair.

With a flath-eaded pick Geordie scrapes the surface away;
with fork and sweat and aching back he turns the soil
and tosses chunks of dirt in the air until all that's left is weed.

He shovels on bought topsoil with grunts and groans,
and rakes in clotted chicken manure fresh and moist,
then levels it as if he were manicuring a croquet lawn.
He bends and bobs, tugging on solitary threads of weed.

The pile of turf stands solid beside him,
his cup of tea with saucer and biscuit
sits on top. He stops, rises and sighs.

To lay the sward Geordie folds each in half and lifts;
he staggers across the dressed rich soil
and kneels, almost collapsing, to lay each weighty turf.
His eyes watery with pain,
his face flushed, his hands black,
Geordie can't fully stand.
He scans his work
and with feeble breaths reaches for his cold tea.

Twenty-four hours in the tropics

Weeping tarmac and
cornflake grass,
precipitation please!

Dusk – discreet drops
a heady aftersmell,
inhaling negative ions.

Stillness at midnight,
cicadas lament
the fleeting sweetness.

Woman with tattoos

On the bus, sitting diagonally opposite a pale woman with tattoos,
the illogical immediate impression, she'd been beaten black and blue,
but after further inspection it was clear all four limbs were fully inked.
Staring dumbly, averting my eyes was not so easy; I, an unpaid critic.
Experience says start with at least a nominally positive statement,
but all I manage is, 'imagine when she's sixty, a poor investment,
envisage the flabby, baggy, crinkled skin crumpled in fading cobalt'.
'I ought to do a bit better. I'm no fuddy-duddy. Sadly, all I find is fault.'

Self-portrait

Asked if I was a glass half full or glass half empty type,
my reply was, *'I'm fine if there is a glass.'*

I seek silence but know there isn't any;
day and night dissolve into each other
with an accompanying symphony
and grass always grows by barleycorns.
Soil effervesces with assiduous fungi
as negative charges tickle senescent silt.
Damselflies create ripples in the air
and earwigs clatter into moist wood;
their frail movements chorus to the grass.
There is an undersong, a veil over silence.

I am a decidedly successful philocalist.
I find beauty in polished floorboards,
and in our Brown Betty teapot with cosy.
In the frantic colours of a tropical fruit salad
and the Wedgwood clouds in sapphire skies.
There's beauty in my softly perfumed lady;
a different sort of exquisiteness again
to narrow English country lanes horseshoed
with overhanging verges and hazel catkins.
I don't manoeuvre to find it; it's there.

History has me like a husk has a kernel.
An awareness of the past sleeps in my marrow,
and I feel like a bead on a thread through time.
I'm au fait with the constant rhythm of migration,
the endless hominal search for freshness.
Between my toes, salt from walking Dogger Bank;
I listen to antler chisels redefining the landscape.
In my nostrils, heady wet tweed from flat caps
and my senses inundated by ships of the line
and, Mum's Linzer Torte permeates the air.

I'm unsure why you want a physical description;
here I am though in the flesh, well almost.
Five foot nine inches with a modest midriff,
tonsured with dove-grey fluffy has-been hair
and hazel eyes, the green of the undergrowth.
Garden variety stature that says very little, but
the quirks which adorn me may stand out.
I have a penchant for double-breasted waistcoats
and specs hanging like a dangling bungee-jumper;
one singularity is my tattoo on the inside, 'Hampshire'.

Strong is how he likes his drinks

Strong is how he likes his drinks, regardless of what.
Builder's brew is the only way he drinks his tea,
the colour of Tamil tea pluckers' betel-stained teeth.
And coffee stronger than an Italian espresso,
thick, black as an alley cat's shadow and bitter.
When it comes to beer, he'll drink just real ale;
Green Jack Baltic Trader at 10% alcohol,
complex and soft as Aslan's mesmeric mane.
Plymouth Gin, Navy Strength, at 57%,
he'll ask for none other,
he likes the earthy root-infused flavours.
On occasions he has absinthe, Green Fairy,
one per cent proof for each of his septuagenarian years,
as if it were a deep warming chlorophyll transfusion.

His emotional palate is quite the reverse,
in poetry, music, art, and the garden, he seeks what's fine,
he appreciates grace and an ethereal element.
He listens to spiders weaving their webs in clickety-click garter stitch
and witnesses them kicking dew drops from dovetailed threads.
Whether the moon is waxing or waning he waits patiently,
and reflects on the nebulous halo around the full moon
as he eavesdrops on the bustling atoms in a caliginous sky.
In the mornings he pre-empts the sunrise and dawn chorus,
and treasures the first rays of sun in absolute awe,
with the moon slinking off like the last guest to crawl away.
When he reads John Clare he reads slowly,
almost fondling the words as if they were three-dimensional,
turning them over and over philosophically.

He wants strength in his sips and refinement in his psyche.

Pint of mild please

I walked into the Jolly Farmer and asked for a traditional pint.
The publican gave me the *Doomsday* book and said, 'Choose your brewery.'
Through the Frankish scrawl I found and mispronounced one
and watched the barman pull a well-aged ale with crown jewels' care.

I enquired if they had old-style bangers, a recipe with pedigree;
by the hand I was led into the garden where the truffles hide in cool repose
and grey-leafed sage grows in the shade of the reliable lovage.
'All these flavours in our pork sausages,' he assured me, with proud eyes.

To top it off, I ordered a slice of bread, from a local bakery, real bread.
A hand beckoned me from out back, where the miller stood at his quern,
his apprentice reground with finer stones and a baker listened to his loaves;
here the skills were harvested from all the generations since the last ice age.

That meal helped me discover more than five mere senses,
from that I was grounded, stilled, euphoric, and I was sated.
It had me waving in the barley field breeze, embracing the uberous soil.
It left me with much to say but blissfully and irretrievably speechless.

Misnomer

Social distancing so-called,
stands Orwellian doublespeak on its head;
what it does is reinvent society.

The art of pickling makes a comeback
and slow cooking simmers
with the kids curious, involved.

Sooty fingers learn to handle charcoal,
on pumice stone coated paper,
bringing light out in carbon shadows.

Dad, who's been reading Helen Steward,
isn't sure if he's locked himself in,
wonders if the lockdown is written in the stars.

And there's more time at the checkouts;
taped crosses one point five metres apart
allow quasi gallows humour, banter and dawdling.

In the shopping trolleys the stuff of hobbies;
seedlings, trowels, yeast, flour, rolls of wallpaper;
husband and wife roll their sleeves up, chatting.

The government in its marketing wisdom
sees social distancing as pinball theory
but what we see is the reseeding of community.

2020 – City centre in absentia

Pavement dancing, in your face, charity fundraising volunteers in pink T-shirts and full youth
peel off and drift away before the morning rush hour has eased into a sloth of retiree drivers.
And when a dead day's done, in twilight shadows, a knee-high pile of *Big Issues* remains untouched, unsold – unseen as the homeless themselves.
The city hall clock knells as if hedged in self-doubt,
while a congregation of white ibises stilt around for the few crumbs remaining.
The travel agent's door as yet unopened, the barber's cut-throat still sits in barbicide and takeaway coffee remains untaken.
What should be is not and what is thought an aberration is.
Dual-drive street sweepers, kerbside crawling at shopping trolley pace, have existential conversations about their contribution to society with gutters offering up meagre tokens of refuse;
they drive past proliferating doorway dwellers in hand-me-down sleeping bags tucking up for quieter nights; cursing, praying, open-eyed snoring.
Empty skies hide estrangement
and the question 'how are you' is laden like no other mundane nicety.
How would Homer with his profound skill in penship historicise this oddness?
From whose perspective will the mainstream memory of this year be cultivated?

Retuned

(A view of nature during the lockdown)

A planeless sky, sweet to the ears.
The unchurned sea returns to blue.

Hedgerows au naturel throb again,
and the stars beckon deep inside.

Wristwatch hours disenthroned;
each passing car now a trespass.

Standing

Our neighbour but one, had his tree felled,
a prodigious structure and sanctuary to many.
He wanted to subdivide his land, sell it off;
there was no division, no sale, just divorce.

It wasn't a crime to cut it down and uproot it,
not in the legal sense, no lawful wrongdoing.
But Christopher Stone argues to the contrary –
he advocates that nature has rights, has standing.

For him a spreading holt is not just timber,
nor is it merely an overused green metaphor.
What he sees is the apparent and the unknown
a breathing sweeping subterranean anchor.

He understands that a tree is not a possession,
it's not built from bricks and mortar or owned,
but ushered into this world with a marvellous lineage
and it confers kinship on those who coexist close by.

This particular tree existed before the suburb did,
it predated even the notion of a name for the place;
it's doubtful it was planted by any mortal being,
how and when its seed was earthed is speculation.

Clearly it was a place of reciprocity, for living beings;
for permanent residents, guardians and free spirits
there was an exquisite integrity, a safe habitual sojourn
for those which were aerial, terrestrial and hypogean.

Birds, both domestic and newcomers, lived there,
they shared the branches with possums and fruit bats.
The tree was busy with scampering legions of fidgety insects,
and spores of mitochondria beneath the ground, in symbiosis.

Travelling roots inched their way gradually forward
with the finer hair-like roots sipping water and nutrients,
and as they did so those solid sinewy massive roots
held the land in sophisticated arboreous coexistence.

None could see, physically at least, the exchange of gases;
for many though, that was simply basic common sense,
that trees take in carbon dioxide from the atmosphere
and exhale oxygen, with humans then respiring, living.

Twinkles of sunlight glistened through dark dense leafage
and between the lighter branches the murmur of wind,
while in the ground a world of complex chemical activity;
for any type of moving creature, that was a place to pause.

That tree was witness to generations galore of night skies,
it doubtless stood unfazed by summer heat or winter rain.
Before a chainsaw destroyed it, ravaged its very essence,
this tree was vital, alive and active in the macrocosm.

Elegant sufficiency

Roquette, a bitterness
balanced by cantles of orange,
and almond sized clods of mango.
A weep of Spanish olive oil,
and roughly hewn *pane di casa* –
a lighter type of sourdough.
Finely sliced, white mushrooms,
delicately arranged in a whorl.

Without salt, without pepper.
just a natural fineness,
not improved by but accompanied by
a glass or two of oaked chardonnay.

Others may add salami or anchovies,
but even without these,
here's a meal bordering the sublime.

It does not take much to be content,
just calmly washing the leaves,
thoughtfully peeling the orange,
savouring each touch, each mouthful.

Change of collar and continent

Grandad wore a tie and waistcoat indoors,
and a flat cap outside, Harris Tweed 6¾.
On Fridays he'd walk the guv'nor to the bank,
iron bar in one hand, reputation in the other.
Conservative to the core, liked the royals;
he'd guide you to his place by the public houses.

Dad, on the other hand, loathed the royals,
and stopped short, just, of singing the red flag.
He too wore a flat cap but jauntily, at an angle,
wouldn't tug his forelock, wouldn't say sir.
cycled the bombed potholes of Shepherd's Bush,
joined the navy aged fourteen, destroyers.

When they met, they'd talk precision engineering,
in inches and fractions, their point of communion.
Dad said, each time, before setting off for Southend,
don't start about the bloody royals, don't forget!
From grandad, a love of waistcoats and fob watches,
from dad, flat caps and happily red, tinged by green.

The fourth-generation male now lives in Australia,
no flat cap, silent on the royals through indifference,
taciturn most of the time and, if talking, soft-spoken.
Splitting image of his grandad, tall and angular, but
less of his great-grandad, the line fizzling slowly out;
London via the Thames estuary to Queensland, PhD.

Changing Services

Across the road the Catholic Church has a neon sign
there's no call to the lapsed to embrace faith again,
it's devoid of pithy wit like the Uniting Church uses.
What it is, on church grounds and so easily visible,
is a constantly changing advertisement, a hoarding
selling the services of several local solicitor's firms
and fast food which somehow isn't junk apparently.
This digital billboard is often a cool sunbed blue,
at other times cardinal red, never a restrained hue,
but then its role is not community art but marketing,
a solitary purpose of shouting down to pedestrians.
The LED element gives its luminosity that little extra,
bluer than the ANZ and brighter by far than Westpac;
it is the complete antithesis of idyllic dark sky parks.
One may conjecture the congregations have dwindled,
the collection basket scantier each time it's circulated;
no doubt the cassock is worn a little tighter now,
and scampering church mice daily given freer rein,
the decanted wine made to go further with prayers.
So, the clergy seeks to hear the rustle of paper notes
to feel the slickness of Australian polymer dollars,
in preference to the tinkle of five-cent pieces and buttons.

Night-time life

Could it be refuted that
a spider on an orange tree
drops its thread at night
for a worm to corkscrew up
onto a shiny dark leaf
to see life from a vantage point.
Or incontrovertibly denied
that cicadas harbour
a northward-bound dream
leaving the tropics behind
to pulsate in Hamburg.
Has it been disproven
that ladybirds don't pose
like Twiggy for fun
but they fear to tread
where no coleoptera has trod.
Indeed, it has not been denied
that damselflies have a hankering
to be vegetarian for a day
and meditate on their DNA
so their kids don't have to prey.

A Brisbane garden is teeming,
with things we six-footers fear,
that make the backyard pulse
like an antediluvian opera.
It's worth remembering
their struggle to live
and their alternative possibilities
like Priscilla Queen of the dessert
or the metamorphosis of Gregor Samsa
or even Joe Bloggs' dreams
of escaping a dreary 9–5.

George Street Wind Tunnel

Left, right, footfalls on the tarmac,
neither conscious nor heard,
as I smash into the wind funnelling up George Street.

At the traffic lights women hold their skirts,
one hand, two hands, tight at the knees,
and all the wonderful hairdos thrash about.

Yesterday's *Big Issue* cavorts
in a whirlwind of dust and leaves
like a khaki whirling dervish.

Then the little green man flashes.
I step off the pavement, head bowed,
smiling, enjoying the battering.

White sesame seeds about two pounds

White sesame seeds about two pounds,
the scales were wonky, balanced with a one-ounce weight,
granulated sugar at a rough guess about eight ounces
(at that time all the bakehouses were in imperial),
bakers' yeast a decent knob, unweighed,
and a couple of gallons of more than luke-warm water.
We tipped it all in and stirred with tender care,
then lidded it and left it well alone.

Being young and pretty stupid (ordinary blokes)
we tried a pared back homebrew, recipe-less.
Each day we skimmed the scum from the top
and slipped a handful of extra sugar in at times.
At first it smelt yeasty, then of ether and never good.
Dad, a polished but amateur vintner, worked in his kitchen
which filled the house with heady elderberry or blackberry
but the muck we'd concocted filled us just with nervousness.

Moses, the baker from Tonga, had a sip in week two,
his face screwed up like a cat's backside, 'more time',
and we left it another week before Dave had a go.
He manned up to the job with gusto and a grin,
his contorted face emitted noises like an Icelandic geyser.
A few more days we agreed, gently removing the froth.
An uncared-for ferment for sourdough would've smelled better.
We kept it warm beside the oven until Friday on week three.

The weekend baking starts late on Friday night,
we'd got the first few runs of white tin loaves out,
then Dave decided a little taster might keep him going.
By 2 a.m. he was wasted, by five our turn,
Moses drank like a fish from five onwards,
and Patrick took the role of generous sommelier.
He gave a running discourse laced with Sinhalese;
by sevenish it was pure gibberish, Moses laughing.

It was probably a few degrees from the news headlines,
'Four die in bakehouse homemade brew', or something,
but no, pungent and rancid it was, but not a killer.
What we did with the sludge afterwards I don't recall,
dodged the neighbours for a few days after though,
they were Bangladeshis running a takeaway shop.
Fumes from our undomesticated vino bettered their Bombay Duck.
Whether it sharpened or deadened my faculties, not sure.

Bury me

Don't bury me with talk of heaven and hell,
don't bury me with priests and prayers,
in fact, don't bury me at all.
Slip me into a brown paper bag and cremate me,
then pay fifty quid to offset my carbon footprint
and sprinkle me round your next transplant
so, I can be immediately useful, like chicken poo.

Go lightly on the watering the first time round,
as lightweight wafers I'd be slush in no time;
great to have a compost purpose but please,
let the night-time dew have the first touch.

Pay no one who talks for a negotiable fee,
write no cheques to the death industry;
spend instead on a case of Merlot.
Then book a week at the opera and gorge on Bizet,
with Green Fairy or gin for the intermission,
and home to feast on the stars.

Stay sober enough to remember the sky,
and tell the constellations about the music;
read Robert MacFarlane to the rising dawn.

I ask you not to dress in black for a day,
not to enquire what medicine could have done;
talk instead in the present tense.
I shall be garnish on your flower beds,
be part of the nasturtiums' anatomy;
back where I came from, and that's fine.

www.ingramcontent.com/pod-product-compliance
Lightning Source LLC
Chambersburg PA
CBHW070334120526
44590CB00017B/2877